S12010

S0-CGP-151

© Franklin Watts 1989

Designed and produced by
Aladdin Books and David West
Children's Book Design
70 Old Compton Street
London W1V 5PA

First published in the
United States in 1989 by
Franklin Watts
387 Park Avenue South
New York, NY 10016

ISBN 0 531 10669 1

Library of Congress Catalog
Card Number: 88-51486

Printed in Belgium

This book is not intended as a substitute for the medical advice of physicians. The reader should consult a physician in matters relating to his or her health and particularly in respect to any symptoms that may require diagnosis or medical attention.

The publishers would like to acknowledge that the photographs reproduced within this book have been posed by models and have all been obtained from photographic agencies.

CONTENTS

Chapter One   The Teenage Parent   5

Chapter Two   Support Systems To Help You Cope   11

Chapter Three Parenting Tips – Your Baby from Birth to 6 Months   25

Chapter Four Your Baby from 6 to 15 Months   39

Chapter Five Your Child from 15 Months to 2 Years   55

Index   62

TEEN · GUIDE · TO

SINGLE PARENT-ING

Herma Silverstein

cop. 1

Consultant: Alan E. Nourse, M.D.

Franklin Watts

New York · London · Toronto · Sydney

Chapter One:
The Teenage Parent

Every year, 192,000 teenage girls become single mothers. Often they must cope with holding down a job or going to school and making a home for their baby. It's not easy, but it can be done.

A high-pitched cry woke Julie out of a troubled sleep. Her alarm clock said 2:00 a.m. She rolled over, hoping the crying would stop. Then she could go back to sleep and forget her worries about passing mid-term exams, paying bills, and finding a better job. But the crying grew into a piercing wail. Julie dragged herself out of bed and shuffled to the corner of the one-room apartment where her 2-month old daughter Kristen lay howling in her crib.

If only Kristen would start sleeping through the night. These 2:00 a.m. feedings were a drag. It seemed Julie had barely fallen asleep again when her alarm would ring, signaling the start of another long, hard day. At least Kristen's food was free – for now. As Julie unbuttoned her nightgown and started to nurse her baby, all the problems she faced flooded her mind.

Her part-time job at the supermarket barely covered a month's expenses. Then there was school. Between taking care of Kristen and working, there was little time left over to study. Her grades had fallen from A's to C's. And just when she'd finally caught up with the bills, Kristen got the flu. Now there was the pediatrician to pay, which would eat into the money she'd saved to buy that new blouse for the spring dance. Julie sighed and stroked Kristen's tiny arm. She might as well forget about the blouse. She wouldn't be going to the dance. She couldn't afford a baby sitter, and besides, she didn't have a date. Her friends didn't ask her to do stuff with them much now that she was a mother.

Julie stared at Kristen, and the love she felt for her baby washed away some of her loneliness. She wouldn't give up Kristen for anything, but sometimes, just sometimes, Julie wished she'd waited until she was older to have a baby. She longed to be with her friends, going to parties and football games, even just hanging out at the mall. After all, wasn't that what most 15-year-old girls did?

Yes, most 15-year-old girls do go to parties and football games. But Julie is not alone in her situation. Every year 1.1 million teenagers in the United States become pregnant. This means that out of every 10 teenage girls, 3 will have a baby before they reach the age of 20. Over half of these girls are not married. Of these 600,000 unmarried teens, around one-half will get abortions. Of the 300,000 remaining, one-third will marry, 4 percent (8,000) will place their babies for adoption, and 64 percent (192,000) will become single mothers.

500,000
Already
married
300,000
Abortions
192,000
Single
mothers
100,000
Marry
8,000 Put
baby up for
adoption

This is what happens to the 1.1 million American teenagers who become pregnant every year.

Like Julie, many of these girls feel trapped, seeing no way out of low-paying jobs that keep them living in poverty and on welfare. Supporting themselves and their children while coping with the stresses of child-rearing, frequently tips the emotional scales from normal anger to rage, so that child abuse results.

Whereas twenty years ago, either marrying the baby's father or placing the baby for adoption were seen as the only solutions to unwed pregnancy, this is no longer true. Today children born to unmarried parents do not carry the stigma of being "illegitimate." And the single-parent family has become just as accepted as the traditional, two-parent family. Nevertheless, many girls still believe that marriage is the only solution to being an unwed pregnant teenager.

However, because over half of teenage marriages end in divorce within the first five years, more and more teenage mothers are choosing to become single parents. These girls believe marriage for the sake of the child is not enough to hold a relationship together. In fact, many parents of pregnant teenagers encourage them not to marry. Sometimes this is because the parents themselves married as teenagers, and they remember the problems early marriage created.

Moreover, while a mother is legally entitled to receive support from the baby's father, in reality fewer than 5 percent of single mothers receive any money from the baby's father. There is no question that it is easier to share the job of parenting with the baby's father. But if a couple feels trapped into marriage, and the husband resents or refuses to help with the baby's care, parenting becomes harder for the woman than if she were raising her child alone.

Even for two people who love each other, marriage is a difficult adjustment. The added pressure of raising a child makes that adjustment harder. If you are considering marriage, ask yourself how much the baby's father will give to the relationship – financially and emotionally. Does he have a job? Will either of your parents help out? Will you be able to finish school? Where will you live? Unless you were already planning to get married before you became pregnant, you might ask yourself why you now want to get married. If the reason is because of the baby, you would be wise to think it through again.

While the future for girls like Julie seems bleak, you do not have to become a negative statistic. Teenage mothers can be good parents. The love and understanding that go into raising a child are not necessarily based upon a parent's age. And there are ways to pull out of poverty. The energy required is double that of teenagers who are not parents, but you can succeed as a teenage parent and achieve your career goals.

Most girls who have succeeded agree that the first and most important step is to finish school. Without a high school diploma, there is little hope of finding a good-paying job with a chance for advancement. And without a decent income, there is little hope of getting off welfare and out of poverty.

Parenting at any age is not easy. But it is especially difficult for a teenager who is also faced with completing school and supporting herself and her child. This book looks at ways teenage mothers can succeed at parenting and become self-supporting.

Being responsible for a baby's life before you yourself are an adult can feel like pushing a grand piano up a mountain. But just as a piano mover would not try to push the piano up the mountain without a strong support system of ropes and pulleys, so you do not have to face raising your baby without a support system of your own.

Chapter Two:
Support Systems To Help You Cope

As a single mother, you have to put you and your baby first. Don't be afraid to seek out agencies and professional people who can help you with aid and advice. That's what they are there for.

At times teenage mothers feel as if their world is caving in. Often they are no longer included in their old group of friends, and do not know where to look for new friends. Even if they do, they usually cannot afford a baby sitter in order to go out with their new friends. A common complaint among teenage mothers is loneliness. How do they manage?

Seventeen-year-old Maria gave this answer: "First you have to believe that you can survive. Then ask questions if you need help – of your parents, your school nurse or guidance counselor, pediatrician, everyone you meet. Never put yourself down. You are worth everything you want to achieve."

Brenda 19, said, "Finish school. I did, and believe me, the hard work was worth it. I never could have gotten the job I have now without my high school diploma."

With their positive attitudes, Maria and Brenda will probably manage just fine. Many other teenage mothers, however, not knowing that there are places and organizations to turn to for help, stay rooted in despair. As Brenda said, finishing your education is a major step in surviving early parenthood.

Educational, Financial and Medical Help

Years ago, pregnant teenagers were expected to quit school. However, Title IX Guidelines of the Education Amendment, a federal law signed in 1975, forbids sex discrimination in any educational institution receiving federal assistance. This means a school cannot keep a student from attending classes or from participating in a school-sponsored extracurricular activity because she is pregnant, married, or a parent. In fact, if you have to be absent from school for a long period of time

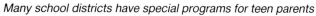

Many school districts have special programs for teen parents

because of pregnancy or childbirth, the school must allow you to return to class at the same grade level as when you left.

So you can stay in school. If, however, you do not want to attend regular high school, many school districts offer special programs for teen mothers and fathers that include day care for infants and toddlers. Besides high school subjects, these programs provide job training and parenting classes as well. An advantage to attending one of these programs is that you can make friends with other teenage parents. And you can learn and share different ways of coping with the special problems of raising a child while still a teenager.

To find out about classes in your city for parenting teenagers, ask your school nurse or counselor, pediatrician, or gynecologist. Or you can look in the Yellow Pages or ask operator information for the number of your city school district office. Someone at the office can direct you to the right person to talk to. Other organizations to contact are your local March of Dimes, United Way, YWCA, La Leche League, Junior League, or Planned Parenthood Association. These numbers can be found in your phone book, or simply by calling telephone information. If one organization cannot help you, ask for the name of an agency that can. Don't take no for an answer.

After you have looked into finishing your education, the next question you will probably ask yourself is, "Where will I live, and how will I pay the rent and other expenses?" If you are not living with your parents (or your husband's parents, if you are married) and you cannot get financial support from your parents, you can apply for Aid to Families with Dependent Children (AFDC) through your local Department of Public Services. AFDC is a government-sponsored welfare program that will give you a monthly cash allowance based upon your financial needs.

At the AFDC office, a social worker will ask you questions about where you live and your income. If you are living with your parents, then they, not you, must apply for AFDC. And if their income is above a certain level, they cannot qualify for AFDC. Be prepared to wait in a long line, as there will be many others ahead of you waiting to see a social worker. After applying, it can take up to thirty days to get approved for AFDC.

Your school counselor or your teen-parenting teacher can tell you where to go to apply for AFDC. Or you can look up the address for the Department of Public Social Services in the white pages of your phone book under County listings. Or simply ask information for the number of the Department of Social Services.

Ask the social worker at the AFDC office about types of housing available. You can also ask any local community agency, such as the Salvation Army, United Way, or a homeless shelter, for help in finding housing. Most apartments require you to pay the first and last month's rent, plus a security deposit. This deposit will be returned to you when you move out if you haven't damaged the property. You might also be expected to pay for gas, electricity, and water. If so, phone the home economics specialist at your gas or electric company and arrange for a free home visit. The specialist will give you tips on how to save on your utility bills. Occasionally you can find public housing projects offered by the government. But usually applications by minors are not considered.

If you live with your parents, there will be some advantages and disadvantages. Among the advantages is the emotional support your parents can give you in raising your child. It is comforting, for example, to have a parent around who can give advice when your baby is sick. It will also be cheaper to live with your parents. And they may be willing to do occasional baby sitting.

The disadvantages to living with your parents often come when your parents and you disagree on how to raise your child. Other problems arise from your parents' tendency to treat you as a child when you are trying to act like an adult mother. For instance, how will you feel if your mother tells your child she can do something you have already said no to? If arguments arise, talk things out and try to reach a compromise. It is also a

Living with parents is an economical solution to housing problems.

good idea to decide who will be responsible for what household jobs *before* you and your baby move in with your parents.

Problems with your parents may also come up when you want to go out with friends and leave your child for your parents to baby-sit. It is smart to work out a plan for how often your parents are willing to baby-sit. But remember, if you leave the decision-making and disciplining of your child to your parents too often, your child will look to your parents for direction instead of to you.

As for your food and medical needs, when you apply for AFDC, you can also apply for Food Stamps and Medicaid (Medi-Cal in California). Medicaid is a government program that provides free health care for you and your baby. You will be given a Medicaid card. Show this card to any doctor you go to. The doctor's office will bill the government for the cost of your health service. Other organizations that can help you find free or inexpensive health care are your local Planned Parenthood Association or your local hospital.

If you plan to have sexual relations with the baby's father or with another boy, you can also get birth control devices for free or at low cost through Medicaid or one of these other organizations. To get the Pill you must have a physical examination and a doctor's prescription. The Pill is considered the most effective contraceptive in use today. Out of every 100 women taking the Pill, about 2 a year may become pregnant.

Another type of birth control that requires a prescription by a doctor is the diaphragm. This is a rubber cup that is put into the vagina. A special cream that kills sperm (spermicide) is squeezed into the cup beforehand. The diaphragm keeps sperm from entering the uterus during sexual intercourse. More spermicide must be inserted each time you have intercourse. And the diaphragm must be left in place for six hours after the last act of intercourse. Each year, of 100 women using the diaphragm, about 19 become pregnant.

Similar to the diaphragm, but smaller, is the cervical cap. Shaped like a thimble, it is made of rubber. The cap is inserted into the vagina after putting spermicide in the cap. It may be worn for forty-eight hours, and while in use it is not necessary to use more spermicide before each act of intercourse. Every year, of 100 women using the cervical cap, about 15 become pregnant.

Other birth control devices, such as the vaginal sponge, vaginal foam, and the condom, do not need a doctor's prescription and may be bought in any drugstore. Condoms are made of rubber and shaped like the finger of a glove. A man rolls the condom over his penis before sexual intercourse. It catches sperm cells and prevents them from entering the vagina. Condoms also provide protection against sexually transmitted diseases such as AIDS.

If you are already raising your child, you know how hard it is to make ends meet. Just imagine how hard your life would be if you had another baby right now. That is why it is important to use some form of birth

A gynecologist can give you information about birth control.

control. Talk about the different methods with your doctor, and then decide which contraceptive seems best for you.

Even with Food Stamps and your cash allowance from AFDC, you may want to add to your income with a part-time job. The social worker assigned to you at the AFDC office may know of some places to apply for part-time work. Be aware, however, that most businesses will not hire anyone under age 16.

You may also qualify for a WIN (Work Incentive) Program. Through this program you can get on-the-job training. WIN participants may get help with child care, transportation, and other job-related expenses while they are in school or in job training. If you are going to school and/or learning a job skill, you may need a day care facility for your child. Ask your social worker at the AFDC office. There may be extra money available for day care. Some teenage mothers trade off baby sitting with each other.

When you talk to your AFDC social worker or other counselor, ask how to get whatever you need. This is no time to be shy. Going to school, arranging for financial help, finding a place to live, and raising a baby may seem overwhelming. But you can succeed, survive, and most important, be a responsible, loving parent.

Coping with Stress and Loneliness

"People told me that being a mother would be hard work, but I never believed them until I had my baby. Peter had colic and hardly slept at all the first three months. A few times I wanted to hit him because all that crying got on my nerves. Then I'd get really depressed. How could I even think of hurting my own baby?"

Barbara, age 14

"When you're a teenage mother, it's like living on an island. You're on land, but you're also floating in the middle of a sea. You aren't a grownup, but since you're a mother, you have to act grownup. Like, it's no fun to stay out late partying with your friends if you have to get up at three a.m. to feed your baby. You can't be half asleep when you're taking care of a tiny baby who depends on you for everything. Sometimes I wish I could run away and hide."

Tina, age 16

At times, all parents wish they could run away and hide. As a teenage parent, you may find the responsibilities doubly challenging. It is hard to take care of a baby when you still feel a need to be taken care of yourself. Many teenage parents feel tied down to feeding schedules and diaper changes. They find it hard to get out of the house since they can no longer leave on the spur of the moment. First they either have to hire a baby sitter, or pack up diapers and bottles and take the baby with them.

This feeling of being tied down is made worse by the normal sadness of "afterbaby blues," sometimes called "post-partum depression," that most mothers feel for about a month after their baby is born. There is a physical reason for afterbaby blues. Your hormones are trying to adjust to your body no longer being pregnant. You'll probably feel better if you talk to someone about your feelings. It will also help relieve the blues if you do not stay cooped up in your house. Go out – with or without your baby.

For some teenage mothers, the normal stress of adolescence, combined with parenting, becomes too much to handle. These girls take out their frustrations on their children. You do not have to become a child abuse statistic. Instead, you can learn ways to cope with the stresses of parenting. When you feel overly tense, calm down by taking a short time-out period from parenting. If you are married, ask your husband to

As a single mother, you mustn't let loneliness get you down.

take over for a while. There is no reason why a father cannot change a diaper or give a baby a bottle as well as a mother. If you are living with your parents, perhaps they would baby sit while you go out for a break.

If you are living alone and cannot afford a sitter, perhaps a neighbor would watch your baby while you walk around the block. Physical exercise helps relieve stress. Try doing sit-ups, knee bends, or jogging in place.

Any time you *are* able to arrange for someone to stay with your baby, use the time to do something special for yourself. Buy a small treat, like an ice cream cone. Window shop, see a movie, or visit a friend. Being good to yourself will allow you to be good to your baby, and thus be a better parent. Even at home you can pamper yourself. While your baby naps, take a bubble bath, paint your nails a new color, or read a book – whatever makes you feel special and calm. For you are still a person with needs and feelings, even when you are a mother.

Some teenagers form cooperative baby sitting groups with other mothers. Each parent chooses a specific day and time each week to baby sit the other children. If there are five parents in the group, this gives the other parents four time-out periods a week. Cooperative baby sitting is especially useful if you are working part time or going to school. You will also make new friends of these parents, which will relieve some of the

Joining a baby-sitting cooperative is a good way to make new friends.

loneliness most teenage parents feel. Many cooperative baby sitting groups also serve a "parents anonymous" function. If your baby has been crying for hours, even though you've done everything to make him comfortable, and now you're about to pull your hair out – or your baby's – you can call another parent in the group to talk to, or even to come be with you until you calm down.

All parents need to get away from their children once in a while. While your baby does need to be cared for all day, if you can let someone else take over for a few hours, even one day a week, you will come back to the job of parenting refreshed and with renewed energy. You will also help your child learn that he can survive without your constant attention – an important first step in your baby's learning to become an independent adult. Do not feel guilty for taking care of your needs. It is a proven fact that people who satisfy their own needs first are better able to take care of others. If you don't, you will only build up anger and be more likely to let out your pent-up frustrations on your child.

Many teenagers attend parent support groups. In these groups, they talk to other teenage parents about the problems of parenting, and share their feelings and ideas on child raising. You will probably find that other parents are coping with the same problems as you. To find a support group, ask your social worker, school nurse or counselor, or a community organization such as United Way for names of groups in your area.

If you cannot find a support group right away, and you feel your anger or frustration getting out of control, you can get help immediately by phoning Parents Anonymous. This organization was started by a mother involved in child abuse. Members of Parents Anonymous meet in small groups with a professional leader. They share their feelings and support each other in finding ways to cope with child rearing. There are now over 800 branches in the United States and Canada. Call information for their number, or if there is no local chapter in your city, ask the operator for a parent abuse hotline number in your area. Or phone Parents Anonymous toll-free at 800-421-0353. (In California, phone 800-352-0386.)

If you are receiving AFDC, ask to see a social worker when you need emotional help. Another source is your county or state mental health association. They can refer you to local counseling programs. Get their phone number from the information operator, or by looking in the white pages under County Listings, Department of Mental Health. Two national family help agencies are Family Service Association of America and Children's Home Society. Each branch of these organizations offers individual and family counseling at low cost, in addition to parent-support groups.

Never feel guilty about asking for help. We all need emotional help at some time in our lives. And the end result – feeling competent and good about yourself, plus having a healthy and happy relationship with your child – will be worth the extra effort.

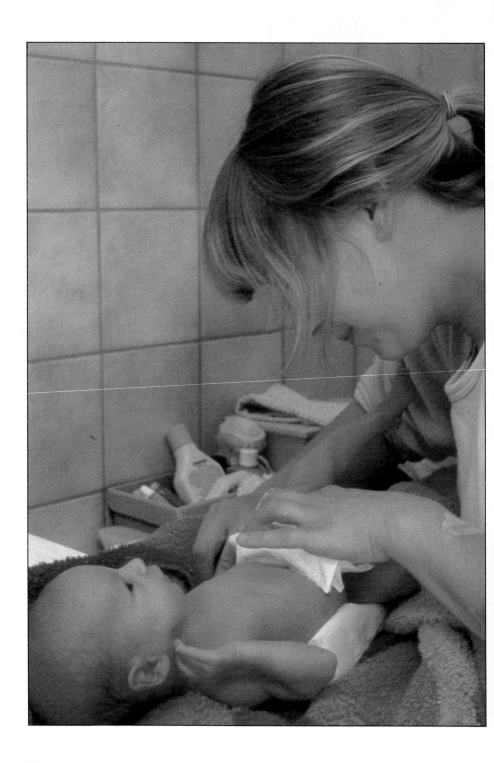

Chapter Three:

Parenting Tips: Your Baby from Birth to 6 Months

When you first bring your baby home from the hospital you might feel unsure about how to take care of this tiny new life — how to hold her, how often to feed her, what to do when she cries. Don't worry, almost all new parents feel this way.

"I thought taking care of a baby would be easy. All you had to do was feed her, change her diaper, and put her back to bed. No way. Every time I'd finish feeding her and start to do something else, like watch TV or talk on the phone, she'd start crying. It was hard to get used to not being able to do what I wanted when I wanted to all the time."

Carol, age 16

"When I brought Jason home from the hospital, I was so scared I'd do everything wrong, and he wouldn't get enough to eat, or he'd get diaper rash, or a stomachache because I didn't burp him right. But after a couple of weeks, taking care of him just came naturally. It was like brushing your teeth. You don't think about how to do it. You just do it."

Tracy age 15

"I wanted to be the perfect mother. I had it all planned out how I'd act, and how the baby would act – sort of like playing dolls. But nothing went like I thought. Instead of waking up every four hours, Becky woke up after two hours. Instead of burping the minute I patted her back, she'd take forever to give one little burp. Then she'd spit up her formula and be hungry again. Finally I gave up trying to be the perfect mother and decided to just be myself and do the best job I could. I'm much happier now. And so is Becky."

Denice, age 17

There is no right or wrong way to parent. The child-raising tips suggested in this book are merely examples of techniques that have worked for other mothers. All the "advice" can be adapted to suit your own life and personality. Fitting a baby into your schedule takes time. The main point is to trust yourself. You have an inborn instinct to mother. The natural care you give your child is more important than whether you pin a diaper on perfectly.

In the first few months of life, colicky babies cry a lot.

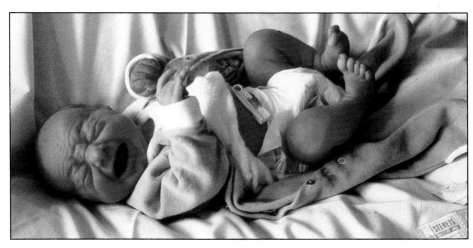

Your Newborn Baby

From birth to 2 months, a baby's needs are mainly to be kept comfortable. Years ago mothers were told to feed their babies on a strict 4 hour schedule. Today, however, most professionals agree that feeding schedules can be flexible. If your baby wakes after 2 hours, and does not fall asleep again after 5 or 10 minutes of crying, it is perfectly all right to offer another feeding, whether bottle or breast. For the first 2 months, most babies wake every 3 to 4 hours if bottle-fed, and every 2 to 3 hours if breast-fed. You will naturally be tired. Try to sleep when your baby sleeps. And do not skip meals. You will feel physically and emotionally better if you get as much rest as possible and eat nourishing meals.

Some babies cry for long periods of time, even when they are fed, dry, or held. These babies may have colic, a kind of stomachache. No one knows what causes colic, but laying the baby across your knees sometimes helps. Colic is wearing on parents' nerves, but it usually ends by the time the baby is 3 months old.

You may be asking yourself whether to breast- or bottle-feed. There are advantages and disadvantages to both. If you breastfeed, this will be the only food your baby needs for the first 5 to 6 months of life. Therefore, breastfeeding is economical. Breast milk is usually easier than formula for the baby to digest, contains substances which help protect the baby from infections, reduces the possibility that the baby will have allergic reactions, and is sterile, always at the right temperature, and ready to serve when baby is hungry.

In addition, breast milk uses the extra fat your body stored for this purpose during pregnancy. Each time you nurse, your uterus contracts, and therefore returns to a normal size faster than if you use formula. If you took prenatal vitamins during pregnancy, continue to take them while breast-feeding. Or ask your druggist for a good multivitamin. These vitamins will help make sure you and your baby get extra nutrition during breast-feeding. You probably will not have to give your baby extra vitamin supplements while breast-feeding. She will get necessary vitamins through your breast milk.

The disadvantage to breast-feeding is that you need to be available to your baby every 2 to 3 hours. Some women, however, stretch this time period by squeezing (expressing) milk out of their breasts into a bottle, or bottles. Then a sitter can give the baby breast milk while the mother has to be out of the house. Expressing will not use up your milk. The more milk that is taken from your breasts, the more milk your breasts will produce. Babies usually nurse for 15 minutes on one breast, and for 10 to 15 minutes on the other. Most women alternate the breast that they offer the baby first at each feeding.

If your breasts get sore, rub them with pure lanolin, an ointment that can be bought at any pharmacy. Sometimes milk will leak from your breasts between feedings. You can either buy nursing pads or put pieces of a clean cloth into your bra to protect your clothes.

To produce enough milk, you should eat a well-balanced diet. Every day you will need to eat at least 3 meals containing fruits and vegetables; milk or milk products; meat, fish, chicken, dried beans, peas, or nuts; and whole wheat or enriched bread or cereal. And you should have 8 to 12 glasses of liquid a day.

If a particular food you eat seems to cause your baby discomfort, such as gas pains, simply cut that food out of your diet. Remember, what you eat or drink will pass into your baby through breast milk. This includes nicotine, drugs, and alcohol. If you are on a prescription medicine, check with your doctor to make sure it is safe for your baby to breast-feed. Women who are taking birth control pills should not breast-feed.

You will know your baby is getting enough milk if she has at least 6 to 8 wet diapers a day, sleeps for 1 to 2 hours between feedings, and is gaining weight. If you have any problems breast-feeding, check operator information for the number of a local La Leche League. This is a national organization for women who breast-feed. Someone there will be happy to give you tips on breast-feeding. You may even want to join the League, as it would be a source for new friendships.

Pause to burp your baby about one-fourth the way through the bottle.

If you do not want to breast-feed, it is perfectly fine to give your baby an infant formula. Your doctor will tell you how much to give your baby at each feeding. In areas with a clean water supply, baby bottles and nipples may be cleaned by washing with soap and water, or by putting the bottles and bottle caps in the dishwasher if one is available. You should wash nipples by hand, however. If your water supply is questionable, or there are flies, ants, or roaches around, sterilize bottles and nipples by boiling them in hot water. Pour the formula into the bottle, put the bottle into a pot of boiling water, and heat the bottle to a comfortably warm temperature. Test the temperature by sprinkling a few drops of formula on your wrist. If the formula feels soothingly warm, it will not be too hot for your baby.

When bottle-feeding, tilt the bottle so that the formula always fills the top of the bottle. This will keep your baby from swallowing too much air. Since some air will get through the nipple, pause to burp the baby about one-fourth way through the bottle. Hold the baby against your chest or in a sitting position in your lap. Then either gently pat the baby's back or rub the back in a circular motion until you hear your baby burp.

Babies need a lot of sucking. Breast-fed babies get most of their sucking while nursing, as they can suck at the breast for as long as they want. Bottle-fed babies, however, should not suck at an empty bottle, as they will fill their stomachs with air that causes painful gas. If your baby shows signs of needing more sucking – by sucking her thumb or fist – offer the baby a pacifier.

During the first 2 months, babies wet their diapers about every 2 to 4 hours. Breast-fed babies may have a bowel movement after every nursing. Formula-fed babies may have 3 to 6 bowel movements a day. Change wet or soiled diapers as soon as possible, since wet diapers can cause diaper rash. You will need about 72 diapers a week, either disposable or cloth. During each change, use a soft washcloth to wash the diaper region with warm water and mild soap. If your baby does get diaper rash, there are ointments and powders you can apply to cure the rash. Because air helps heal diaper rash, let your baby go without a diaper as much as possible.

Bath water should be warm, not hot. **Remember to support baby's head.**

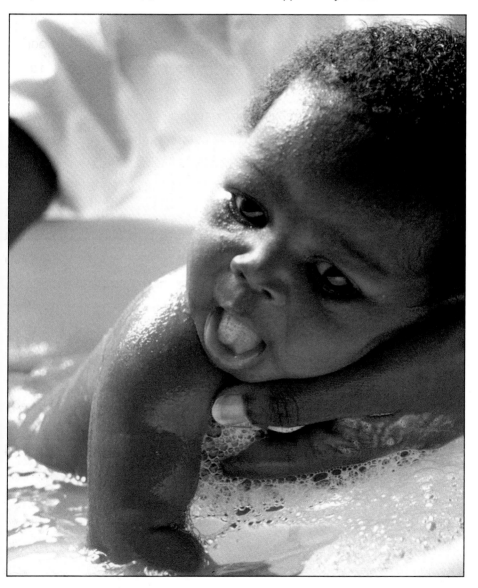

Until the stump of the umbilical cord falls off, about a week after birth, do not tub bathe your baby. Use a cotton ball to pat a little rubbing alcohol around and under the cord to keep it clean and help dry it up. If there is any bleeding or foul-smelling discharge from the cord, phone your doctor. Even after the cord falls off, you do not need to bathe your baby every day. But do keep the baby's head clean, or "cradle cap," a dry, scaly condition like dandruff, might result. If "cradle cap" does occur, wipe the head with a small amount of baby oil. The condition should disappear within a few weeks.

When bathing your baby, first test to make sure the water is not too hot by dipping your elbow in the water. If it feels warm, it is fine for your baby. Rest the baby in the crook of one arm, then gently lower her into the tub or sink. Use your other hand to lather the head and body (do not use soap on the face), then rinse thoroughly. Wrap your baby in a towel and pat dry. Baby powder and lotion are not necessary. In fact, powder may irritate the baby's lungs. Do not use cotton swabs to clean ears, nose, or navel. Use the corner of a washcloth instead. Bath time is a good opportunity to "play" with babies, by talking or singing, as they kick and move their arms and legs.

Until about 18 months, babies have a "soft spot" on the top of their heads where the skull has not grown together yet. The soft spot makes it possible for the bones in the head to change shape in order to fit through the birth canal. Do not be afraid to touch the spot: it is protected with a tough membrane.

If you have a boy, and he was circumcised, (a simple operation to remove the foreskin from the penis), put a small amount of petroleum jelly covered by a strip of gauze on the penis to protect the circumcision from infection until it heals. This operation was once thought to be necessary for cleanliness. Today, however, there is no medical reason for circumcision, and the matter is left up to the parents. If you are undecided, talk to your doctor. If your baby is not circumcised, do not forcibly retract the foreskin. It will retract naturally in time.

Most babies go to the doctor for their first checkup around 4 weeks after birth. This is a good time to ask any questions you have about caring for your baby. Keep a record of how long your baby nurses at each breast, or of how often and how much your baby eats at each feeding. Your doctor will want this information so that he or she can advise you how to adjust your baby's feeding schedule.

When taking your baby in a car, be sure to buckle her into a crash-tested car seat. Even a strong adult cannot hold a baby safely in a car crash. The safest place for an infant seat is the middle of the back seat of the car. When deciding how to dress your baby for the outing, remember that babies need the same amount of clothing as you. If it is hot outdoors, a diaper and undershirt will do.

By about 6 weeks, most babies can follow an object with their eyes. Be sure to talk to and cuddle your baby when you feed, change, or bathe her. Babies hear very well at birth. Soon your baby will recognize your voice and touch, and will respond by cooing and moving arms and legs. Around 2 months she will smile at you.

Every child needs to be smiled at, talked to, touched, and held. This is how the process of bonding occurs. Bonding means that you and your baby grow to feel you belong to each other. Do not be afraid of spoiling your baby if you pick her up whenever she cries. Babies cry because they are uncomfortable. When parents respond to a baby's cries, they are helping their child develop a sense of trust in the parents, which will then be carried over into trusting other people.

During these first 2 months, get to know your baby. Respond to her needs, talk to her, and hold and kiss her. You may feel nervous at first, and worry about doing everything right. But there is no need to feel extra stress. Relax and enjoy your child. Remember, besides food, a baby's most important need is to be loved.

Your Baby from 2 to 6 Months

By the time babies are 2 months old, they have personalities all their own. Your baby's eyes will follow you across the room. He will laugh and make gurgling sounds, as if he were trying to talk. It is important to give your baby a chance to see and touch things. Hang a mobile over his crib, for example.

Even at this age, you can begin reading to him. Ask your children's librarian to recommend books for your child's age. Studies have shown that children who are read to from an early age learn how to read faster once they begin school. Children also learn faster if they are talked to, played with, and held, rather than left alone in a crib or playpen for most of the day.

Your baby should begin getting immunization shots at 2 months.

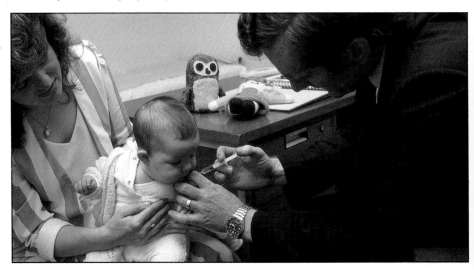

Between 2 and 5 months, babies become aware of their bodies. They stare at their hands and feet as if they had found a treasure. Your baby will start to roll over from back to stomach and vice-versa. He is curious about the world around him, and reaches out for anything within eyesight. This is the time to put a stuffed animal, a rattle, or other infant toy into the crib so he can practice his new skills.

You will help your child learn self-esteem if you praise every accomplishment, no matter how small, and answer gurgles as if he were really talking to you. If he reaches for the stuffed animal, cheer him on. He will learn to trust that you'll listen to his needs, and you will build an open relationship with your child.

At 2 months old, your baby should begin getting immunization shots against diseases. These immunizations are free at any health department. Be sure to keep a record, signed by whoever gives the shot, of the date and name of each injection. You will need this record in order for your child to enter kindergarten.

The first immunization is called a DPT, because it protects against diphtheria, pertussis (whooping cough), and tetanus. Three DPT shots are given, spaced 2 months apart. The fourth DPT is given between 15 and 18 months, and the fifth shot between 4 and 6 years of age. A booster for diphtheria and tetanus is given every 10 years thereafter.

In addition, your baby will need a series of vaccines against polio. The first 3 are given by mouth at 2, 4, and 6 months. A fourth is given at 18 months, and a fifth between 4 and 6 years of age. At around 15 months, your baby will also get a vaccine against measles, mumps, and rubella (German measles).

By about three months, your baby will probably start sleeping through the night, giving up the 2:00 or 3:00 A.M. bottle. Most babies still get cranky once in a while. It is normal for you to feel frustrated or angry at your child when he cries for a long time no matter what you do to quiet him. It is important that you do not let angry feelings become angry actions. Try to stay calm, as babies imitate their parents. If you are unhappy, chances are your baby will be, too. If he hears you yelling all the time, he will learn to yell for his needs.

You can save money by making your own baby food.

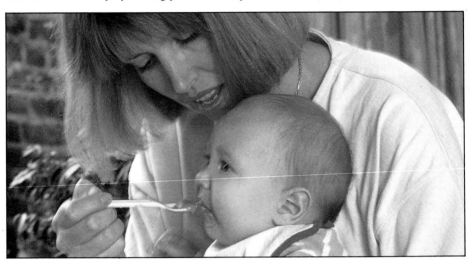

Around 4 months, you can start adding solid foods to your baby's diet. Eating habits – and eating problems – are started in infancy. So the more nutritional foods you feed your baby, the more likely he is to eat healthily throughout life. Do not feed babies puddings or other baby food desserts. They do not need them. Read the labels on baby food jars to make sure you are buying fruits, vegetables, and meats that do not have cornstarch, salt, sugar, or refined starch added.

When starting solid foods, offer your baby milk first to satisfy his hunger. Then three-fourths way through the feeding offer the solid food. Most doctors recommend starting with precooked baby cereal. Begin with rice cereal. Do not give your baby mixed cereal. If he has an allergic reaction, you will not know which ingredient caused the allergy.

Mix the cereal with normal formula or breast milk. Start with only a teaspoonful of cereal and work up to two or three tablespoons. If your baby refuses to eat the cereal, sometimes mixing a little strained fruit into the cereal helps. Do not force him to eat. Instead, wait about a week, then try again. Do not be discouraged if at first most of the solid food lands on his chin rather than in his mouth. He was born knowing how to suck, but he has to learn how to chew and swallow solid foods. Be sure to praise your baby for every morsel he swallows. Do not feed any solid food through a bottle or infant feeder. Your baby needs to learn how to eat from a spoon, so he can taste the flavor and texture of different foods.

After your baby has been on cereal for a few weeks, strained fruit and fruit juices may be added. (Orange juice should not be given until a year old.) Then strained vegetables are added, and finally strained meats. Your pediatrician will tell you when to add each of these.

It is less expensive to make your own baby food. Just cut up baby's portion of whatever meat and vegetables you prepare for yourself. Then mash it through a hand-held sieve or strainer. Add a little water if too thick. Fruits such as apples, plums, or apricots should be peeled, then boiled until soft. Use ¼ cup of water to one cup of fruit. Afterwards, mash the fruit through a strainer or sieve.

A word about thumb sucking: most babies suck their thumbs a few minutes before feeding. If your baby sucks his thumb the minute feeding is over, or between feedings, it means his sucking need has not been satisfied. Giving him a pacifier usually helps.

From now on, your baby will be becoming more of a distinct person, with his own individual personality. The process of child development is fascinating to watch, and being a parent gives you a front row seat.

Chapter Four:
Your Baby from 6 to 15 Months

Your baby is now developing quickly and can be weaned. She will soon start teething, sitting up, playing with food, crawling, and eventually walking.

When your baby is 6 months old, you can start switching her from breast or bottle to a cup. This is called weaning. While you continue to nurse or bottle-feed, also offer sips of milk from a cup at each meal. By 9 months, encourage your child to hold the cup herself. Increase the amount of milk in the cup as she seems willing to take more. Next leave out one daily breast-feeding or bottle, and give her only the cup at that feeding. A week later, leave out another breast- or bottle-feeding. And in another week offer only the cup.

If your breasts become too full during weaning, let her nurse for 15 to 30 seconds to relieve the pressure. However, the less you nurse, the less milk your breasts will produce. When you stop nursing altogether, your breasts will soon stop producing milk completely. Most babies are ready to drink only from a cup between 9 and 12 months.

At six months many babies can sit up by themselves. Now you can start bathing your baby in a regular bathtub. Put some floating toys in with her. Never leave her alone in a tub. Babies can drown in only an inch of water.

Your baby can now be put into a highchair for meals, and start eating finger foods. These are foods that babies can pick up with their hands, such as graham crackers, pieces of banana, slices of raw apple, and bits of cooked vegetables, meat, or potatoes. If you are buying baby food, you can switch to Junior foods. Handling finger foods prepares babies to feed themselves with a spoon.

Be prepared for a mess. Babies love to smear food on themselves and the highchair tray. Playing with food is part of babies' satisfying their curiosity to explore new tastes, textures, and smells. At this time, your baby may be ready for a three-meal-a-day schedule. A sign that she is ready for a three-meal schedule is if she has a good appetite at one meal, but has little appetite at the next meal.

Around 7 months of age, most babies get their first tooth. By 1 year, they usually have 6 teeth, 4 up, 2 down. Many babies get fussy when their teeth cut through their gums. They may try to bite everything they hold. A teething ring, frozen in the freezer first, or teething lotion rubbed on the gums, will help ease the pain.

If you are breast-feeding, baby may bite your nipples. If so, remove your breast from her mouth and say "No." Even if she cries, wait a few seconds before offering the breast again. This remedy is an example of the "behavior modification" type of discipline, in which you give your child natural consequences for her negative action. (You are really saying, "If you bite my breast, your food source will be taken away as a consequence.")

The best way to take care of baby teeth is to offer water between meals to rinse milk and food particles out of the mouth. Do not give your baby a bottle to drink by herself at bedtime. Milk has natural sugar in it and will damage teeth if it stays on them all night. In fact, never give a baby a bottle to take to bed. She could choke.

Between 6 months and 1 year, babies begin to crawl and to pull themselves into a standing position. Standing gives them a real challenge, since they now have to learn how to sit back down. You may hear your baby cry out as if she were in terrible pain. You run into the room and find her standing up holding tight to the side of the crib or playpen. You sit her down, and she stops crying only to pull herself right back up. Fortunately this up and down game ends after a week or so, when she will learn how to sit down.

When your baby is about one year old, she will take her first step.

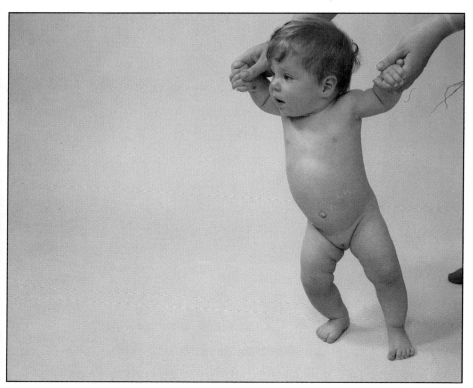

The next step in baby's development is to move around a room by holding onto pieces of furniture. Soon she will have enough courage to stand all by herself. At about a year she will take her first step. Then it is only a matter of a few weeks before she starts walking. All this moving about means that from now on your baby can touch any object within reach. And if she can touch it, she most likely will try to put it into her mouth.

Now is the time to childproof your home. Put breakable or sharp objects high up, out of baby's reach. Put blind plugs (available at any hardware store) into all unused electrical outlets. Put a gate at the top and bottom of stairs. When your baby learns to open doors, attach hook and eye type fasterners high up on the door to keep baby out of rooms you do not want her in. Childproof your kitchen by putting dangerous objects such as knives inside a locked cabinet. When cooking, turn pot handles toward the back of the stove. Baby will be less likely to grab the pot and pull it over on herself.

Put child-proof fasteners on cabinets containing medicines, detergents, insecticides, and other poisonous substances. Many house plants are poisonous. Keep them out of baby's reach. Be sure any paint you buy is lead free. If your baby swallows something poisonous, save the container to take with you to the hospital. Phone a hospital emergency room or your local Poison Control Center for advice on first-aid treatment. This number is listed at the front of every phone book. Copy it and paste it on every phone in your house or apartment.

Do not put a pillow in baby's bed, as she could bury her head in it and suffocate. Cut up and throw away plastic bags from dry cleaners. If a baby pulls a plastic bag over her face, she could suffocate, because the plastic clings to her face and cuts off breathing. If you are anywhere near a swimming pool, lake, or ocean, do not take your eyes off your baby for one second. Drowning is one of the major causes of early childhood deaths. If you can afford it, you may want to give your baby swimming lessons. Check with your local YMCA or Department of Recreation and Parks (both listed in the phone book) about swimming classes for infants and toddlers.

Even after you childproof your house, never leave your baby alone in a room. Putting a child in a playpen is all right for some of the time. However, it has been proven that children who are penned up in a playpen too long have slower intellectual development, because they do not have enough opportunity to explore their environment.

What emotional changes are taking place in your baby between six and twelve months? The main change is that your baby will want to have more independence, but at the same time keep the security she enjoyed as an

Babies are naturally curious and will want to explore. When your baby is old enough to move around, it's time to childproof your home. Some potentially harmful items are large plastic bags, uncovered electrical outlets, pots on the stove, insecticides, household cleaners, and other poisonous substances, and crib pillows.

infant. This attitude can be seen in the way she squirms out of your arms, or insists on holding the bottle herself. Yet whenever she is tired or frustrated, she returns to infant behavior, such as sucking her thumb, stroking a stuffed animal or blanket, or rocking back and forth on her knees. Frequently babies become so attached to a blanket or stuffed animal that they want to carry it at all times. They usually outgrow this dependency between 2 and 5 years of age.

Another new behavior that appears around 8 months of age is a sudden fear of strangers. When grandparents or baby-sitters come over, your baby will bury her head on your shoulder and refuse to be held by anyone other than you. This behavior is a sign that your baby is learning whom to trust. She trusts you. It will take time to trust others.

Still another new "trick" of baby's is a result of her learning about the law of gravity. While in her highchair, she drops a rattle, a pacifier, or other object. She looks to see where it went, and discovers it landed on the floor. When you pick up the object and give it back, she will drop it again. This game will continue for as long as you are willing to play. Let her switch a light off and on. She will be delighted when she realizes she can make something happen.

You do not need to buy toys. Rather, give her plastic measuring spoons, cups, pots, or pans. She'll enjoy banging them and filling and emptying them with other toys. Be sure to praise her when she plays by herself. That way, she won't learn that to get your attention she has to whine or misbehave. But also play with her. Babies love a game of chase, in which you crawl after them across a room. A good game to play is "peek-a-boo." Put a blanket over your head, then pull it off and say "peek-a-boo." This simple game helps your child learn to believe that when you leave, you will come back.

It is important to talk to your baby to help her develop language. As you dress her, name the articles of clothing you put on. While bathing her, name the parts of her body. As she crawls around a room, name the different furniture she passes. Read to your baby as much as possible. Picture books are perfect for this age, since you and baby can point to objects or animals and say their names. Many libraries have story hours for young children, in which toddlers come to hear a story read. This is a great opportunity for your child to learn to get along with other children, and for you to meet other mothers.

Around 9 months, bedtime may become a problem. Your baby is so interested in what is going on around her that she does not want to go to bed. Most parents find that setting up a bedtime routine helps. This routine can include putting on pajamas, brushing teeth, a drink of water, and a story. Having a special stuffed animal to take to bed also makes bedtime easier. Make a point of tucking her in and kissing her good night. It is all right to leave a night light on and the door open. Then say "good night" firmly and walk out of the room.

No one ever said that raising a child was easy. And you are probably finding that out about now. But the effort of creating a safe environment in which your child can explore the objects around her will be worth the trouble when you see your child developing into a bright, happy person.

Your Baby from 12 to 15 Months

"If you think getting up in the middle of the night to give your baby a bottle is hard, just wait until your child starts walking. Then you have to watch them all the time. Kerry is fourteen months old, and she's into everything. She grabs anything – a tablecloth, lamp cord – to pull herself up with, and she puts whatever she can pick up into her mouth."

Jennifer, age 16

Because toddlers do "get into everything," and have to be watched at all times, most parents find this stage hard to manage. A toddler's memory is just starting to develop. Therefore, they do not remember that yesterday you said not to touch the vase on the coffee table. Slapping their hands when they pick up a forbidden object does little good, and only teaches children that it is all right to hit someone when they do not do what you want.

The healthy approach is to remove your toddler from the dangerous or breakable object and suggest a safe toy or activity instead. Because toddlers are extremely curious about the world around them, they can be easily distracted from one object or activity to another. When he wriggles and squirms while you change his diaper, give him a toy to hold to distract him from wriggling.

Save your "No's" for your child's really dangerous behavior, such as running into the street. If he hears No constantly, he may think you mean "Don't explore" or "Don't try new activities." And when you do say No, be sure it's for something that will always be forbidden. A child will be confused if one time he is allowed to pick up a particular object, and the next time he is told No.

Around 12 months, many toddlers learn to climb—onto a chair, a kitchen counter, or up stairs. Give him an opportunity to practice this new skill. Allow him to go up and down stairs, or climb onto a sturdy chair while you watch closely. A favorite activity at this age is emptying things – drawers, cabinets, trash cans, bookshelves. Allow him to empty the contents of at least one drawer or cabinet. You can also fill a box or plastic container with blocks and other toys and let him empty it. (A word of caution: Check your child's stuffed animals and remove any eyes, ears, bells, or ribbons that could be pulled off and put into baby's mouth.)

Toddlers love to play outdoors. If you do not have a yard, perhaps there is a public park close by. This is the perfect age to play in a sandbox. He will love having a pail to fill up and empty. When children start walking outside, they need shoes. There should be ½ inch of space between their big toe and the end of the shoe. You will think all you do is buy shoes, since toddlers' feet grow so quickly.

Most children start learning to talk by the end of the first year. And one of the first words they learn to say is "No," especially at mealtime. If you insist that your child eat, he will probably become more determined not to. The best solution is to let him eat the amount he wants.

Because toddlers like to explore, they have to be watched at all times.

Reading to your child is important to his language development. Children who are read to develop better speaking abilities than children who are not exposed to books. Around 15 months, your toddler will say such one-word sentences as "Up," to mean, "Pick me up," or "Down," to mean, "Put me down."

What is going on emotionally in your toddler? Most likely he wants to stay close to you and cries or screams when you leave him with a sitter. Let him take his time getting to feel comfortable around baby sitters by having the sitter arrive a half-hour before you leave. Do not leave your child with the sitter after he is asleep. Waking up to find a stranger in the house instead of you is frightening and teaches him he cannot trust you not to sneak off while he sleeps.

Around 15 months, most toddlers can undress themselves. Be prepared. Once they master this skill, they may show off their new skill by stripping at the most inconvenient moments − when you are in the supermarket, for instance.

Because toddlers get into everything, it may be tempting to let television become a baby sitter. But watching TV is passive learning. Children learn better from actively participating in learning experiences. Sitting in front of a TV does not allow your child to develop the muscles that running, jumping, bending, and standing do. The side vision (peripheral vision) of children who watch a lot of television is less clear than for children who read. Reading forces you to move your eyes from side to side, whereas you just stare straight ahead while watching TV.

You will probably be taking your child out more often now that he is a toddler. This exposure to other people and places means he may pick up infections such as colds and viruses more often. Fever is one of the first signs that a child is sick. Call your pediatrician if the thermometer reads more than 99 degrees when taken under the arm. If your doctor prescribes medicine, ask if you should give the medicine until it is all gone, or only give it until the symptoms disappear. Most antibiotics, such as penicillin, should be given until the bottle is empty.

You can also help bring baby's fever down by giving him a cool, lukewarm bath. A cold-water vaporizer will help him breathe more easily if his nose is stopped up or he is coughing. Be sure to give your child plenty of liquids when he has a fever, diarrhea, or is vomiting. If he does not want to swallow juice, try popsicles, soup, jello, weak tea, or watermelon.

A good way to check if your child is sick is to take his temperature.

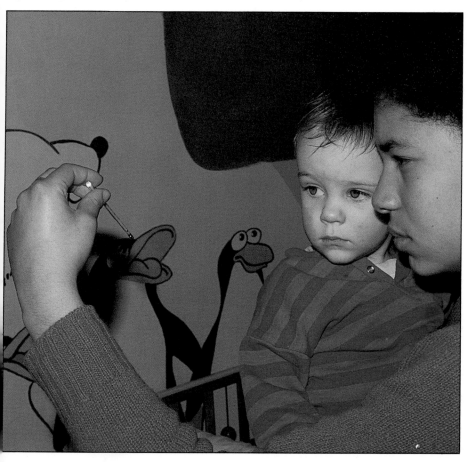

When your child reaches the toddler stage, it is time to add discipline to your care-taking responsibilities. Some people think discipline means punishment. But discipline really means teaching. You are teaching your child to get along with others and to respect others' rights and belongings. Using discipline takes a lot of energy and willpower. It is much easier to let your child do what he wants than it is to take the time to remove him from the negative behavior or situation.

Think of discipline as setting limits on your child's behavior. Children actually thrive on limits. Because they count on you to take care of their needs, they expect you to stop them from hurting themselves or others, and will feel frightened and insecure if you do not. Discipline will be easier if you get your child to *want* to do what you want him to. For example, if you want him to put his toys away after playing, he will be more willing if you do not order him to clean up. Instead, make it a game. You might say, "Let's put your toys in the wagon, and I'll help you haul them to the toy box."

You will also get better results if you say what you want him to do instead of what you do not. For instance, instead of saying, "Don't touch that lamp," say, "Leave the lamp on the table." If possible, give your toddler a choice. For instance, instead of saying, "Drink your milk," say, "Do you want your milk in the big glass or the little glass?"

You will also be less frustrated when your child refuses to do something if you never allow yourself to become involved in a control struggle. A control struggle is when you insist he do something, and he refuses. At this point never threaten – "if you don't mind me, I'll do such and such." Most children consider threats as dares. They will test you by doing the forbidden activity to see whether you will make good your threat.

If you do threaten, follow through on your threat. Otherwise, your child will never take you seriously, and thus not mind you unless he wants to.

Discipline is setting limits on your child's behavior.

Two phrases that work with toddlers are, "You need to – " and "You may not – ." By setting firm limits, you are teaching your child to take responsibility for his actions.

Think of "logical consequences" for both positive and negative behavior, instead of dealing out a punishment that has nothing to do with the negative behavior, such as being sent to his room for not picking up his toys. A "logical consequence" for not putting dirty clothes in the hamper would be to tell him that only clothes in the hamper get washed.

"I" statements are another method of getting your child to do what is necessary. If something is not done, say what you will do. For example, if your child refuses to take a bath, say, "I will not allow anyone who is dirty to ride in my car. So if you feel you don't want to take a bath, I will get a baby sitter to stay with you while I go to the store."

Hugging is an excellent way to comfort your child.

Keep in mind that positive behavior comes mostly from reward and encouragement, not from punishment. Your baby smiles at you, and you smile back. He will smile a lot more because he is being rewarded by your smile. Rewards for positive behavior should not be candy or extra privileges. A hug, a smile, or your praise are the strongest rewards, for children truly want their parents' approval.

Spanking is not an effective punishment. Besides teaching the child that hitting is an acceptable behavior when you are angry, you may also get out of control in your anger and hurt your child physically, and thus emotionally. If you childproof your house, and at the same time arrange the surroundings so there is a minimum of restrictions, there is no reason to spank a child under two years of age.

If your child becomes so angry or frustrated that he cannot stop his destructive behavior no matter what the logical consequences, try the "time out" method of discipline. Put your child in a chair and tell him he needs to take some time out to get back in control. Set a kitchen timer for one or two minutes, and tell him he cannot get out of the chair until the timer goes off. Stay in the room with him. If he refuses to sit, gently hold him in the chair. Using the timer puts the problem where it belongs – off your shoulders and onto your child's, who is responsible for the actions that put him in the chair in the first place.

There will be times when you are tired, and your patience will wear out. You may yell at your child, and all your efforts at discipline fly out the window. You are perfectly normal. Do not feel guilty. Acknowledge that you are human, not a robot, and you make mistakes just like everyone else. Tell your child that you are upset today, and it isn't his fault. Then give him an extra hug.

There is no such thing as a bad baby. There is only bad behavior that will hurt the baby if it is permitted. Do not give up if your child repeats the forbidden behavior a few times. All children test their parents' rules at every stage of development. Testing is how they learn what is real and what is not. This "reality testing" is how they become whole individuals with their own egos.

So remember, you are punishing the *behavior*, not the *child*. If you put a "good" or "bad" label on the behavior, not on your child, you will not destroy his self-esteem, and he will become a self-disciplined, and thus happier, adult.

Chapter Five:
Your Child from 15 Months to 2 Years

The "terrible twos" – that period from about 15 months to 2½ years – will try any parent's patience. Your child will be trying to become more independent, and in the process will be more frustrated and more likely to have temper tantrums.

"Timmy is like two people in one. He's either real good or a real brat. His favorite word is **no**. Whatever I tell him not to do, that's what he does. If we go to the store, he runs down the aisles touching everything. If I try to hold him, he screams. It's really embarrassing. People look at you like you're this awful mother because you can't make your kid behave. At those times, I feel like punching Timmy in the face. But the next minute he'll do something really neat – like run to me with his arms up calling, "Mommy," like I'm his favorite person in the whole world. Then all I want to do is hug him, he's so cute."

Heidi, age 17

The toddler stage has been compared to adolescence. For just as teenagers want to become more independent, yet still have the support of their parents, so toddlers try to move away from depending upon their parents for survival, but at the same time want to be sure the security they felt from their parents as infants is still there. As young as they are, toddlers still want to make some decisions for themselves. They want to control what they eat, when or whether they use the bathroom, and when they go to bed. That is why a toddlers' favorite word is usually "no" at this age. Saying "No" is a way of saying, "I want to do it my way."

The period beginning at around 15 months and lasting until the middle of the second year has been called "the terrible twos." Handling a strong-willed toddler can be a struggle. It is like flying a kite. You unravel the string more and more as the kite flies higher, but you also know that you can reel in the string if the weather gets too windy.

During this stage, your toddler will have some temper tantrums. These outbursts are the result of frustration. When she tries to dress herself, she may accidentally pull the sleeve over her head, or she tries to put a puzzle piece in a space that doesn't fit. She does not have the language ability to talk about her frustration, so she screams and kicks. When her screaming gets out of control, she is throwing a temper tantrum.

What should you do? Spanking or punishing in other ways is not the answer. For at this moment, she has no control over her behavior. The best tactic is to ignore a tantrum. You can go into another room or, if you have a lot of will-power, stay in the room with your toddler, and pretend to be involved in another activity until she stops screaming.

Another tactic is to become a human security blanket. To do this, sit down behind her, and wrap your arms around her chest, pinning her arms to her sides. Cross your legs over her legs. She will struggle to get out of your hold, but do not give in to her demands. Just quietly say an "I" sentence: "I won't let you hurt yourself or anyone else, so I will hold you until you can get control of yourself again." She may yell and cry, but inside, she is relieved to know you won't let her desire for independence go farther than she can handle.

Toddlers have temper tantrums when they become frustrated.

What is happening emotionally to your baby now? The toddler stage is considered by many child experts to be the most important learning period in a person's life. How well your child develops socially and intellectually now forms the basis for future development in these areas. Allow her to continue satisfying her curiosity, and to use her big body muscles in running, jumping, throwing, and climbing.

If bedtime is a problem, that bedtime ritual you started when she was an infant can now be revised to help settle her down. Before bed is a good time for a bath to relax your toddler. If she has her two front teeth, you can help her brush them. Next, let her pick out a story for you to read. Then tuck her in with her favorite stuffed animal, say good night firmly but lovingly, and walk out. Your tone of voice should be confident, giving her the message that bedtime is just as much a part of her day as play time.

For mealtime, toddlers can eat the same foods you eat. Just cut it into finger-sized pieces. Do not urge your child to eat more than she wants. Overfed children become fat adults. Do not offer sweets. For between-meal snacks, offer juice, graham crackers, milk or fruit. To avoid eating problems later in life, try not to show any emotion whether your child cleans her plate or barely touches her food. Remember, she is not a good girl because of what she does or does not eat.

Around this time, your toddler will want to use a spoon to feed herself. Let her have a few minutes at each meal to practice this new skill. Spoon-feeding is difficult, and she may give up if you come to the rescue the minute she has trouble getting the spoon to her mouth. When she has learned to finish her favorite food with a spoon all by herself, it is time for you to quit feeding her at all.

Your child is now ready to use outdoor playground equipment, such as swings, seesaws, slides, and jungle gyms. Be sure to play with your toddler every day, even if it is just for half an hour. And during that half-hour, give her your full attention. Experts say it is the quality of time you spend with your child that counts, not the quantity. Follow-the-leader is a fun game now. Indoor play at this age includes coloring, stacking toys, musical instruments, building blocks, and simple puzzles.

If your friends bring their children to play, remember that toddlers do not yet know how to share their toys. If your child grabs another's toy, wait a minute to see if they will resolve the problem themselves. If your child keeps grabbing the other's toy, or hits the other child, remove your child from the scene and offer her another toy.

Children at this age also love to play pretend by dressing up in Mother's or Daddy's clothes, especially hats and shoes. As part of this play, your child may invent an invisible friend or pretend her stuffed animal or doll is her playmate. Go along with her pretending; she will give up her invisible friend when she is ready, usually around the time she starts kindergarten. It is normal for boys to play with dolls, too. This helps prepare them for becoming fathers later in life.

Reading with your toddler is a fun way to learn new words.

During this time your toddler will start saying more words. She will mispronounce a few. Do not correct her speech. Instead, pronounce the word correctly when you talk to her. Children learn faster if they are not criticized for their mistakes. Your encouragement will help develop her self-esteem and confidence. By the end of the second year, most children can speak in two-word phrases. But not all children begin to talk at the same age, so don't worry if your child does not talk much. Toddlers are starting to understand the concept of time now, so talk about what happened yesterday, and what you have planned for tomorrow.

If you have been reading to your child all along, chances are she is talking more than she would have otherwise. Your local library can be your best friend right now. Picture books will still delight her, as will Mother Goose rhymes, fairy tales, and animal stories.

During a toddler's second year, the first and second molar teeth come in. Some children get extremely fussy at this time, because their gums hurt as the teeth cut through. Give your child something cold to bite on, such as an ice cube. Or rub her gums with your finger. Now is the time to give your toddler her own toothbrush, and to start a regular routine of brushing, at least twice a day.

About the time their toddler is talking more and doing more grown-up activities, many parents believe their toddler should be potty trained as well. But most child care experts agree that potty training should not even be brought up until a child is over 2 years of age. The best way to train up until that time is to let your child see other people in the family using the toilet. Instead of pressuring your child to use the potty, you are letting her natural desire to mimic convince her to want to use a toilet.

All the do's and don'ts of parenting make the job seem overwhelming at times. But remember that there is no wrong or right. Loving your child and using your common sense are the best parenting tools. Much of parenting is on-the-job-training. You will learn by doing.

The more you realize that you can meet your child's needs to be fed, changed, bathed, and disciplined, the more confidence you will have in parenting. By talking to your baby, reading to her, and responding to her needs, a bond of trust will develop that will endure throughout each stage of her life. Just by raising their children parents become the expert on their own child's well-being. After you learn the basics of parenting, the truth is that no one else can know what your child needs better than you.

cop. 1

Toilet training should start sometime after your child's second birthday.

Index

Page numbers in italics indicate illustrations.

Abortion/adoption, 6–7
Aid to Families with Dependent Children (AFDC), 13–14, 16, 18, 22–23
AIDS, 16
Attention, 34–35, *34*

Baby sitters, 14–15, 18, 21, *21*, 48
Bathing the baby, *31*, 32
Bedtime, 44–45, 58
Behavior modification, 50–53, *51–52*
Birth control, 16–17, *17*
Bottle feeding, 30
Breast feeding, 27–29, 39
Burping the baby, *29*, 30

Child abuse, 7, 18, 22, 52–53
childproofing the home, 42–43, *43*
Circumcision, 32–33
Climbing/crawling, 41, 46
Colic, 18, 25
Cradle cap, 32
Crying, 5, 18, 25, *26*, 36

Day care, 13, 18
Diaper changing, *24*, 30–31
Discipline, 40, 50–53, *51–52*
Divorce, 6, *7*
Dressing up, 59, *59*

Expenses, 5, 6
Exploring, 46–47, *47*

Fear: of being a mother, 18, 25; of strangers, 44
Feeding, 6, 25, 32–33
Food Stamps, 16

Housing, 14

Illness, 14, 48–49, *49*
Immunization shots, 35
Infant care: at birth – 6 months, 25–48, at 6 – 15 months, 39–54 at 15 months – 2 years, 54–61

Job, 5–7, 12–13, 18, 21

Language development, 44–45, 47–48, 60
Loneliness, 6, 11, *20–21*, 21

Medicaid, 16

Post-partum depression, 18
Potty training, 60, *61*
Poverty/welfare, 7, 8, 9

Rolling over, 35

School importance of, 8–9, 12, 13

Sharing, 59
Sitting up, 40
Sleeping, 6, 35
Soft spot, 32
Solid foods, 36–37 *36*, *38*, 40, *54*, 58
Standing, 41
Statistics, 6, *7*
Stress, 9, *10*, 11–25, 19–20
Support systems, 9, 11–25

Teethings, 40–41, 60
Temper tantrums, 56–57, *57*
Toys/games, 44

Umbilical cord, 32
Undressing themselves, 48

Vitamins, 27–28

Walkings, 42, 44–45
Weaning, 39

Photographic Credits

Cover and pages 4, 15, 21, 26, 31, 36, 52, 54 and 59: Anthea Sieveking/Network; pages 10, 49 and 57: Vanessa Bailey; page 12: Laurie Sparham/Network; pages 17, 24, 41 and 61: Zefa; page 20: Spectrum; page 29: Janine Weidel; pages 34, 47 and 51: Camilla Jessel: page 38: Marie-Helene Bradley.